EN226 - Solve That Crime
Enslow Publishers   6 Volum
Set Price: $110.69   Page
Reading Level: 5th Grade, 6t

Interest Level: Primary, Middle, Secondary,
These 48-page books are high interest titles written for reluctant
readers. What better way to get students reading than through
forensics. Each book describes a key technique and includes
activities similar to those used by crime-scene investigators. Includes
sidebars, highlights of actual cases, and describes the forensic
techniques used to solve the crime.

Title	Code	List Price	Our Price	Copyright	Prg.
At the Crime Scene!	EN033733	$23.93	$18.45	2010	A
Bones Speak!	EN033771	$23.93	$18.45	2010	A
Counterfeit!	EN033788	$23.93	$18.45	2010	A
Crime Under the Microscope!	EN033740	$23.93	$18.45	2010	A
Crimebusting!	EN033757	$23.93	$18.45	2010	
Virtual Crime!	EN033764	$23.93	$18.45	2010	A

SOLVE THAT CRIME!

At the Crime Scene!

Collecting Clues and Evidence

Carol Ballard

Enslow Publishers, Inc.
40 Industrial Road
Box 398
Berkeley Heights, NJ 07922
USA

http://www.enslow.com

Copyright © 2010 The Brown Reference Group Ltd.

This edition published in 2009 by Enslow Publishers, Inc.

Library of Congress Cataloging-in-Publication Data

Ballard, Carol.
  At the crime scene! : collecting clues and evidence / Carol Ballard.
      p. cm. — (Solve that crime!)
  Includes index.
  Summary: "A look at how evidence is found, collected, and analyzed at a crime scene"—Provided by publisher.
  ISBN-13: 978-0-7660-3373-3
  ISBN-10: 0-7660-3373-2
  1. Crime scene searches—Juvenile literature. 2. Forensic sciences—Juvenile literature. 3. Criminal investigation—Juvenile literature. I. Title.
  HV8073.8.B275 2009
  363.25'2—dc22
                                   2008033306

Printed in the United States of America

10 9 8 7 6 5 4 3 2 1

To Our Readers: We have done our best to make sure all Internet Addresses in this book were active and appropriate when we went to press. However, the authors and the publisher have no control over and assume no liability for the material available on those Internet sites or on other Web sites they may link to. Any comments or suggestions can be sent by e-mail to comments@enslow.com or to the address on the back cover.

♻ Enslow Publishers, Inc. is committed to printing our books on recycled paper. The paper in every book contains between 10% to 30% post-consumer waste (PCW). The cover board on the outside of each book contains 100% PCW. Our goal is to do our part to help young people and the environment too!

For The Brown Reference Group plc
Project Editor: Sarah Eason
Designer: Paul Myerscough
Picture Researcher: Maria Joannou
Managing Editor: Miranda Smith
Editorial Director: Lindsey Lowe
Production Director: Alastair Gourlay
Children's Publisher: Anne O'Daly

Photographic Credits:
Shutterstock: Olivier Le Queinec front cover; Corbis: Andrew Brookes/Flirt 16, Robert Sciarrino/Star Ledger 28; Dreamstime: Shariff Che'Lah 40; Fotolia: CatPaty13 26, Haemengine 21, Stepanov 17; Getty Images: Bulent Kilic/AFP 12; Istockphoto: Stefan Klein 6, Rich Legg 7, Paul Tessier 27, Jaroslaw Wojcik 41; Science Photo Library: Michael Donne 13, Mauro Fermariello 34, John Mclean 39, Philippe Psaila 4, 10, Jim Varney 9; Shutterstock: Nick Alexander 36, Gualtiero Boffi 32, Katrina Brown 24, Kevin L Chesson 30, Dhoxax 37, Romanchuck Dimitry 22, Elisanth 15, Laurence Gough 45, Stephen Kiers 29, Emin Kuliyev 31, Andre Nantel 35, Olivier Le Queinec 14, Serg64 43, Kenneth Sponsler 33, Dale A Stork 18, Stephen Sweet 5, Leah-Anne Thompson 42, Jason Vinz 23, Klemens Waldhuber 19; Topham Picturepoint: The Image Works/Bob Daemmrich 8.

Contents

Hunting for clues

Criminals commit most crimes on the spur of the moment. They do not think about the clues they leave behind. A footprint in a flowerbed, a fingerprint on a door handle, and a strand of hair on the carpet—these are just some of the clues that can lead the police to a criminal. Some clues can help them figure out when and how the criminal committed the crime. By looking at all the clues, the police can sometimes piece together exactly what happened.

4

Forensic examiners collect evidence marked with a numbered tag at a crime scene.

Forensic scientists bag the clues found at a crime scene so they can examine them back at the crime lab.

Different kinds of clues

Different crimes provide different kinds of clues. The clues might come from:

- environmental factors, such as the times of high and low tide, or river currents
- digital equipment such as computers and cell phones
- footprints and other marks made by a criminal
- fibers from clothing
- weapons, such as bullets and knives
- fingerprints and bite marks left by an attacker
- biological evidence such as hairs, blood, or saliva
- insects such as maggots on a body
- chemicals such as poisons, drugs, or cleaning fluids.

Forensic scientists examine all the clues and provide the police with as much information as possible.

Analysis

After the crime scene has been examined, samples are taken to the forensic science laboratory for analysis. Eventually, the forensic scientists at the laboratory send their reports to the police. These should help the police make sense of what happened. In many cases, the clues allow them to identify the criminal. Arrests can be made, and the court process can begin.

At the crime scene

When the police are called to a crime scene, they seal off the most important areas. These areas must be left untouched until they have been searched for clues. This is because clues could be spoiled or destroyed. For example, picking up a cup at a crime scene might smudge a fingerprint left by the criminal. Walking over soft ground could destroy a footprint. Hair from a police officer or an innocent person could be confused with one left by a criminal. To avoid losing or spoiling any clues, tape is tied around the area to mark off the perimeter.

6

Police tape seals off a crime scene so that the area is left undisturbed.

This is the primary crime scene of a murder investigation. The outline of the victim's body is marked in chalk.

IN DEPTH

Detailed procedure

When police and crime scene investigators arrive at a crime scene, they follow certain steps:

1. Interview the first person at the scene, other witnesses, and possibly the victim to find out what happened.
2. Examine the crime scene to establish the layout and identify possible clues and evidence.
3. Photograph and record the crime scene. All the details, including the exact positions of the victim and any evidence, must be carefully noted.
4. Process the crime scene to identify and collect physical evidence for analysis at a forensic laboratory.

Crime scene investigators

Special officers called crime scene investigators collect evidence at the crime scene. They wear protective body suits so the crime scene does not become contaminated. They find the clues by examining the site very carefully. If a crime took place outside, weather can destroy evidence. Tents are sometimes put up over outdoor crime scenes to help protect them.

Primary and secondary crime scenes

There are two types of crime scenes. A primary crime scene is one where a crime has actually occurred. For example, this might be the crime scene where a burglary took place. A secondary crime scene is one where a suspect has been, either before or after the crime was committed.

➡ A police officer
talks to a witness
to find out about
a crime that has
taken place in
the area.

8

Interview

Witnesses can tell an investigator a great deal about a crime.
Did they see anything unusual? Did they notice any strangers?
Was anyone seen running away? Have there been unusual cars
or bikes outside? Did they hear arguing? Did an alarm
go off? Neighbors, local shopkeepers, passers-by, friends,
and family members—all of these people may have useful
information that can help the police with their enquiries.

Examine

Many crime scenes are inside buildings, so the criminal must
have gotten in somehow. Are there any signs of a break-in,
such as a broken window or damaged door lock? If not,
could the criminal have had a key or been let in by the victim?
Are there any signs of how the criminal left the building?

If the crime scene is outside, the crime scene investigator makes
a quick check for any disturbance on the ground. Are there any
footprints or tire prints? Have any plants been disturbed or
damaged? Has anything been dropped or left behind?

Photograph and record

Whether the crime scene is inside or outside, the crime scene
investigator must record any possible clues and evidence so
they can be examined in detail later. Photographing the crime
scene is the best way to make a permanent record.

Photographs show where everything is and record important information such as whether a door is open or closed and the exact position of a victim's body. Close-up photographs can also reveal detailed information about small areas. These might show the exact position of evidence, such as a bloodstain on a wall. Other methods used for recording the crime scene include video recording, making notes, and sketching.

Process

Once everything has been recorded, the crime scene investigators start to uncover all the clues. Some items are put in bags and taken back to the crime laboratory for investigation. For example, hairs and fibers found at the crime scene must be studied under microscopes. Other evidence must be processed at the crime scene, such as fingerprint evidence that is revealed when investigators apply a powder to door handles and other surfaces.

A forensic examiner carefully dusts an empty bottle with powder to reveal fingerprints left on the glass.

TRUE CRIME...

Hair evidence

In October 1994, a woman was stabbed to death. At the crime scene, investigators found a bloody baseball cap. It contained a few hairs. Police had several suspects, and samples of their hair were examined. None matched the hairs in the baseball cap. After more than a year, the murdered woman's son-in-law boasted that he had killed her. Police arrested him. When they examined a sample of his hair, they found it matched the hair found in the baseball cap at the crime scene. The son-in-law was sentenced to life in prison.

10

rime scene investigators search every part of a crime scene in great detail to look for clues. The search often starts in places that a suspect is most likely to have touched. In a burglary, for example, the criminal will probably have touched surfaces such as cupboards, doors, and windows.

A forensic examiner bags a gun found at a crime scene. It will be analyzed back at the crime lab.

TRUE CRIME...

Hit-and-run

A car driver hit a pedestrian and drove off, leaving the victim to die. Police arrested the suspect and searched his car. Forensic specialists examined the car's paint. It was blue metallic paint, with a yellow primer underneath. They then carefully scraped the victim's clothing and collected the scrapings on a large piece of white paper. When they examined the scrapings under a microscope, they found paint flakes that seemed to match the paint on the car. To be certain they were the same, the scientists analyzed the chemicals in the paint from the car and the paint from the scrapings. They were identical. This evidence helped to prove that the suspect was the hit-and-run driver.

Types of evidence

There are two main types of evidence. Physical evidence includes fingerprints and footprints, guns and bullets, and marks made by tools and other weapons. Biological evidence includes body fluids, such as blood and saliva, as well as marks made by tools and weapons.

Using Luminol

Luminol is a chemical that reveals traces of blood that people cannot see. Luminol glows bright blue when it reacts with blood. The chemical is not enough to confirm the presence of blood. Other tests prove if it really is there. This is because Luminol also glows blue when it mixes with other chemicals, such as bleach.

IN DEPTH

Light work

Investigators use a special type of light source at crime scenes. Certain chemicals are applied to the surface that is being looked at. If the surface is then viewed with the light, evidence such as fingerprints and bloodstains show up. This technique can even reveal writing that has been scribbled over.

Forensic examiners search the site following an explosion outside a fast-food restaurant in Istanbul, Turkey.

Search patterns

If a crime scene covers a large area, searching must be particularly methodical so that no vital clues are missed. Investigators have developed several different search patterns, to make sure every search is thorough and complete:

Spiral in: A crime scene investigator starts at the edge of the crime scene. The investigator walks around it slowly in smaller and smaller circles, until he or she reaches the center. The investigator's steps make a spiral pattern.

Spiral out: The crime scene investigator starts at the center of the scene. The investigator walks around it slowly in bigger and bigger circles, until he or she reaches the edge. Again, the steps make a spiral pattern.

Lines: The crime scene investigator walks backward and forward in straight lines until he or she has covered the entire crime scene. The steps make straight lines.

Parallel lines: Many crime scene investigators walk next to each other in straight lines from one side of the crime scene to the other. Together their steps make straight lines.

Grid: The crime scene investigators cross the crime scene in one direction. Then they turn to walk at right angles to their first crossing. Their steps make a grid pattern.

Zone: The crime scene is divided into smaller areas. Each crime scene investigator is given a small area in which to search.

Crime scene investigators take photos of a murder victim to record the exact position of the body.

IN DEPTH

Using photographs

Investigators can take close-up photographs to record the evidence at the scene. This is a simple way to show other people, such as a judge and jury members, exactly what the crime scene looked like. For example, a close-up photo of drops of blood shows how many there were and how they were scattered. Investigators use photographic scales in the photo next to the evidence to give an idea of the size of blood drops.

13

There's been a murder!

A murder has been committed. The body has been removed by crime scene investigators and they are now searching the area thoroughly. These are the clues they have found at the scene.

1. Broken glass on the floor below the window suggests the suspect smashed it to get into the crime scene. The glass is examined for clues.

2. There are drops of blood on the window frame. Bloodstains must be photographed and samples taken to the lab for analysis.

3. A paper cup may have traces of saliva on it. The DNA can be extracted from it and analyzed.

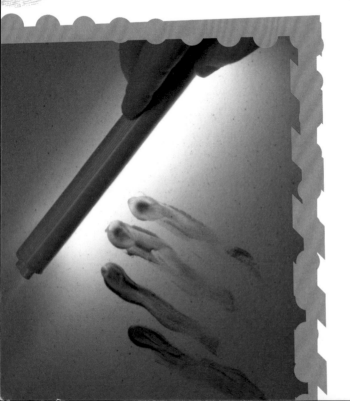

A special light reveals bloody fingerprints on a wall. Do they belong to the victim or the killer?

Does this button belong to a jacket worn by the killer? What type of jacket is it from? How did it fall off?

4. There's a footprint on the windowsill. Taking photographs and using an electrostatic dust lifter will help to match it to actual shoes.

5. Could there be a fingerprint on the doorknob? Dusting with powder will reveal it. Then the print can be lifted with sticky tape and attached to a card. Back at the lab it can be compared to prints of known criminals.

6. Could there be fibers on the rug? Any that can be seen can be picked up with tweezers. Then the rug can be vacuumed to pick up any that are too small to see with the naked eye.

7. There is a bullet stuck in the door frame. It must be removed very carefully. It could provide vital evidence about the type of gun from which it was fired.

8. There are two glasses on the table. Are there any traces of saliva that could be analyzed? This could help identify the people who were drinking.

S ome evidence is fragile. It may spoil or be easily destroyed, so crime scene investigators collect it first. Once this is done, they can collect other, more durable evidence.

Hairs and fibers

Any hairs or fibers are picked up carefully using tweezers and put into sealed bags or containers. Some surfaces may be vacuumed so that nothing is missed. A clean bag is used for each area, so that investigators know exactly where every tiny scrap was found.

A crime scene investigator picks up a hair using a pair of tweezers. The hair will be analyzed back at the crime lab.

A suspect's sneakers have left an impression in the mud. Forensic examiners will take photographs of the footprint and make a cast to record the evidence.

Solid objects

Investigators take photographs of items such as broken glass, bullets, and weapons. They put them into plastic bags so they cannot be damaged, and attach labels so they can be identified when they are examined back at the lab.

Making casts

If a footprint is found in mud, investigators take photos of it. Next, they make a permanent model of the footprint, called a cast. To do this, the crime scene investigators mix casting material and water to make a dough like mixture. They pour this material into the footprint in the mud. The cast is left until it fully hardens. It is then carefully lifted out, put in a box, and taken back to the lab.

IN DEPTH

Body fluids

Some items may contain traces of body fluids, such as blood or saliva. For example, a dirty glass could have traces of saliva on it. This could yield a substance called DNA. This is found in every part of the body and every person's DNA is unique to them. This means that DNA found at a crime scene can be used as good evidence to link a person to a particular place. Items that might yield traces of body fluids are gently wiped with cotton swabs to soak up any fluid present. The swabs are taken back to the crime lab for analysis.

Fingerprints

Suspects leave fingerprints on many different surfaces. Some are visible, such as those left by a blood-soaked hand on the smooth surface of a wall. Fingerprints can also be left on a softer surface, such as soap. An indentation might be visible, but not the fine details. Fingerprints left by sweat on a smooth surface cannot always be seen by the naked eye. Investigators use other techniques to see these prints.

A fingerprint is lifted from a surface using sticky tape. The print will be transferred to a special type of card to make it more visible.

Finding prints

Crime scene investigators look for fingerprints on surfaces such as doors and handles. It is highly likely that a suspect has touched these surfaces. Sometimes, shining a bright light on a surface can make the print visible. It becomes difficult to see when the light is switched off. Methods have been developed to make a permanent record of prints like these.

Fingerprints can be used to confirm the identity of a suspect.

IN DEPTH

Collecting prints

Investigators use one of several techniques to make fingerprints more visible:

Powder can be brushed onto a surface. It sticks to the print, making it visible. The powder can be black, silver, or some other color that contrasts with the surface. A photo of the print is taken. Transparent cellophane tape is placed over the print. The tape is removed, lifting the print with it. The tape is then stuck onto a card of a contrasting color to the powder.

Chemicals such as iodine, ninhydrin, or silver nitrate can be used to reveal prints on porous materials. The chemical can be sprayed onto the surface of the material, or the material can be dipped into the liquid chemical. The chemical makes any fingerprints become visible.

Fumes, such as those from a special glue, can make a print visible without damaging the object on which it is found. The glue is heated on a metal plate. The plate and the object on which the print is found are put into an airtight container. The fumes from the glue react with the fingerprints to make them visible.

Clues in environment

The environment can provide a lot of information about a crime. Sometimes it can confirm that a suspect's story is true. Sometimes it can prove that a suspect is lying. It can also help the police to locate a body or other items.

TRUE CRIME...

Pine tree seeds

In 1960, the body of Graeme Thorne was discovered. On the body, forensic examiners found seeds from a rare pine tree. There were no pine trees of that type near the place where the body was found. The seeds appeared to be a clue to the investigation. Police searched for a pine tree that could have yielded the seeds. They found one in a garden nearby. They also found that the mortar between the bricks of the house matched mortar dust found on the body. With these separate clues, police were able to identify and convict the murderer in this case.

Weather evidence

Weather experts know what the weather was like at a certain place and time. This can help the police to confirm a suspect's story. For example, a suspect may say that her car skidded on ice. The expert may say that it was too warm for the road to be icy. This would suggest the person is lying.

Soil evidence

Soil has different features depending on its source. A suspect's shoes may have soil traces. Analyzing the soil can then provide evidence that the suspect has visited a place.

Tides and currents

If a body is thrown into a river, the current will carry it away. Knowing the speed and direction of the current can help the police in two ways. If they know where and when something entered the river, it can help them find it. If they find the body, it can help them figure out exactly where it was thrown in.

Tides can provide similar information. High and low tides occur twice a day. The timing of the tides can provide useful information in a police search.

Plant evidence

Traces of plant matter can be analyzed and linked to places where that type of plant grows. For example, finding hazel pollen on a person's clothes shows that they have been in an area where hazel trees grow. Plants at the crime scene can also yield clues. They may have been trampled on, or low branches may have been broken.

Traces of tiny pollen grains on a person's clothes can reveal where he or she has been.

21

EXAMINE THE EVIDENCE

Soil types

Collect a few samples of soil from different locations, such as a field or a garden. Put each soil sample in a separate plastic bag. When you have collected them, tip each soil sample onto a tray and compare them. Differences such as color, texture, and the presence of stones or dead plant matter can reveal differences between soil from different places.

Digital evidence

Computers reveal all sorts of information that can help the police solve a crime. Detectives may need to search laptops and PCs, as well as places where data may be stored, such as on CDs, memory cards, or the internet. Depending on how many officers are available, and how much material must be searched, the length of an investigation can vary from a few days to several months.

The forensic examination of computer equipment is central to many criminal cases.

IN DEPTH

Hiding information

Information is often hidden to make it more difficult for police to find. Files are protected by passwords. They can also be encrypted, so that they can only be read using the software that decodes them. People may delete files to prevent them from being read, but it is almost impossible to remove all traces of them. Experts can still access the files. Some criminals use "anti forensics" software. This makes it much more difficult for detectives to access the information on the computer.

⬆ **Criminals may encrypt files to prevent the police from looking at them.**

A careful process

Forensic examiners locate all the files on the computer. They track web sites and e-mails. They keep a record of everything that they do so they can prove that their actions have not changed the computer in any way.

Other digital clues

Other electronic equipment can yield information. Cell phones store contact details. Companies that make the phones keep records of where the phones are when calls are made. These details provide important clues for police investigating a crime.

IN DEPTH

On the internet

Internet companies keep detailed records about their customers' internet use. This includes details of all the web sites they visit, how often they visit them, and how long they spend on each site. This information can be extremely useful to crime investigators. For example, a computer that has been used to look at the web sites of terrorist groups may link the owner to terrorist activities.

Clues from marks

Different types of marks reveal important information about a crime. Footprints, bullet holes, and tire and tool marks are all vital evidence of what happened and who was involved.

Footprints

Footprints are left in one of two ways. If someone stands in something soft, such as sand or soil, their weight pushes down. The shape and distinctive tread patterns of the shoes become visible. If someone treads in something sticky, wet, or powdery, it clings to their shoes. When they walk on another surface, a footprint is left behind. Forensic scientists take photos and make casts of these footprints to record the evidence.

Tires leave tracks in the sand. The forensic experts take photos to keep a record of the tire tracks.

Tire tracks

Tire tracks are left in the same ways as footprints. Driving through mud leaves tracks in the mud. Driving onto a road transfers some mud to the road, again leaving marks. Photos and casts of these tracks can be compared with the tires of a suspect's vehicle.

Tool marks

Criminals use tools to break into houses and vehicles. A tool makes a mark when it moves across a surface. Several factors affect the mark that is made. A screwdriver and a knife have differently shaped edges. which leave differently shaped marks. The surface that the tool is used on is important too, as a tool leaves a bigger mark on a soft surface than on a harder surface. Another factor is the force used to make the mark. The stronger the force, the bigger the mark is likely to be. The way the tool is moved also affects the type of mark made. A single stabbing movement makes a narrow, deep mark. A sideways movement makes a long, shallow scratch.

EXAMINE THE EVIDENCE

Look at your footprints

Have a close look at your own footprints. Put a clean sheet of paper on a hard floor. The paper should be bigger than your feet. Put on a pair of shoes with a clear pattern on the sole. Go outside and stand in a muddy area, then put one foot on your paper. Press down firmly, then lift your foot. You should have a clear footprint on your paper. You could try this with some friends and compare your prints. Can you identify each person's shoes?

25

Bullet holes

Bullet holes can help forensic scientists to figure out from which direction the bullet was fired. Scientists can figure out the height the gun was at and the height of the person holding it when it was fired. Sometimes a bullet is found in a wall or doorframe. Digging it out might damage it, so a chunk of the wall or frame is cut out, with the bullet still in it. The bullet is removed carefully at the crime lab.

Clues from weapons

Finding a weapon can be a major breakthrough in solving a crime such as murder. The weapon can often reveal a lot of information.

Weapons of all kinds

Many different objects can be used as weapons. Some criminals carry weapons with the intent of committing a crime. Some everyday items are picked up on the spur of the moment and used as weapons. For example, a baseball bat can be grabbed during an argument and used to hit someone.

Using weapons to catch a criminal

Weapons can help the police to identify a criminal. This might be directly, for example, through records that shops keep when people buy guns. Sometimes a criminal may leave evidence, such as a fingerprint or a trace of DNA, on a weapon dropped at a crime scene.

Forensic experts can tell a lot about the shape of a knife used by a criminal by looking at the victim's stab wounds.

Using ballistics

Forensic ballistics is the study of ammunition and the marks guns make on the ammunition when it is fired. The barrel of a gun makes scratches and marks on every bullet that is fired. Most guns make patterns on the ammunition that are different from other guns. Investigators may be able to match a bullet to the gun that fired it. Recently, though, some people have questioned whether ballistics evidence is always accurate.

Weapons can also link a criminal to a crime. It is often possible to identify the gun from which a bullet was fired. If the police have a bullet from the crime scene, they can examine their suspect's gun. If the two match, it is likely that the suspect was involved in the shooting.

Stab wounds can reveal a lot about the type of weapon that caused the mark. The shape of the blade, including its width and length, can be discovered from the wounds. This can help police to narrow down the search for the weapon. It can also be used to determine whether or not a particular weapon could have caused the injuries.

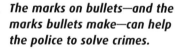
The marks on bullets—and the marks bullets make—can help the police to solve crimes.

27

TRUE CRIME...

Murder

Ballistics evidence was first used in a murder case in 1902. The expert witness, Oliver Wendell Holmes, Jr., fired a bullet from a suspect's gun into a wad of cotton. He then examined the bullet and compared it to the bullet that had killed the victim. The marks on the bullets were identical. The court found the suspect guilty of murder.

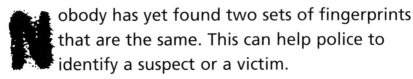

Fingerprints and bites

Nobody has yet found two sets of fingerprints that are the same. This can help police to identify a suspect or a victim.

Fingerprints

Crime scene investigators collect all the fingerprints they can find at a crime scene. They also take prints from suspects and see if they match those from the crime scene. Matching prints is good evidence that the suspect was at the crime scene. Police keep records of the prints of known criminals on a computer database, for use when fingerprints are found at a crime scene.

A police officer takes fingerprints from a suspect. The prints will be stored on a computer database.

Animal teeth

Animal bite marks can be used to help solve crimes. Every type of animal has a differently shaped jaw and different numbers and arrangements of teeth. For example, a cougar's jaws and teeth are different from a wolf's jaws and teeth. People can be killed by wild animals. By examining the bite marks, investigators can find out what type of animal was responsible for the death. They may even be able to tell if the animal was young or old.

Forensic experts compare bite marks to dental records to identify a suspect.

29

If police do not already have a suspect, they can try to match the prints with those on the database.

Bites

Bite marks on skin can be recorded and compared with photographs of a suspect's teeth. They can also be compared with a cast of a suspect's bite. The features that are compared include the size and shape of the jaw, any missing teeth, and teeth that are broken. This provides the evidence that will help to identify or clear a suspect. It has not been scientifically proven that a person's bite mark is unique, but many researchers believe that may be true.

EXAMINE THE EVIDENCE

Make your own fingerprints

You can make your own fingerprints. Rub a soft pencil on a piece of paper to make a dark area. Rub one of your fingertips over this until it becomes gray. Then carefully apply a piece of no transparent just cellophane tape to your fingertip. Pull it off slowly and stick it onto a piece of plain white paper. Your fingerprint will show up clearly!

Biological evidence

Biological evidence at a crime scene comes from many different sources. Some evidence, such as hairs and spots of blood, are obvious. Other evidence may be less obvious, or even invisible to the naked eye, but it is no less important.

Sources

Where should a crime scene investigator look for biological evidence? The chart on the next page shows a few possible sources, exactly where to look on those sources, and what type of evidence might be found.

The saliva taken from a suspect could match saliva found at a crime scene.

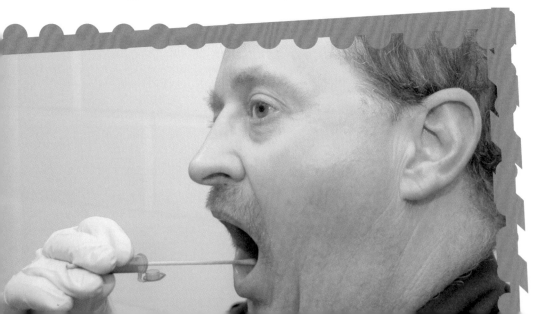

Serology

The study of blood is called serology. Blood contains serum. It also contains red and white blood cells. Serum and red blood cells can provide useful information about a blood sample:

- **Serum** can help identify a person. Scientists study substances called antibodies. The body makes these substances to fight disease. If they are found it shows that the person has had a particular illness at some time in their life. This can be crucial in identifying an individual. Even identical twins, with identical DNA, will have different serum antibodies.

- **Red blood cells** can be used to find out a person's blood group. Human blood belongs to one of four groups: A, B, AB, or O. It is also classified as either Rhesus Positive (+) or Rhesus Negative (-).

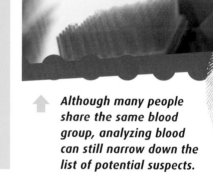

31

Although many people share the same blood group, analyzing blood can still narrow down the list of potential suspects.

Source	Where will the evidence be?	What evidence could be found?
dirty clothes	anywhere on the surface	sweat, traces of skin, hairs
used stamp or envelope	licked part of the stamp	saliva
hat	inside	sweat, hair, dandruff
bottle, cup, or glass	around the rim	saliva, sweat
glasses	nose pieces, ear pieces	sweat, traces of skin
cell phone	anywhere on the surface	sweat, skin, saliva

DNA evidence

DNA evidence was first introduced in the 1980s. Since then it has been used in many different countries to solve a wide variety of crimes.

What is DNA?

Gathering DNA evidence involves complex scientific processes, but the idea behind it is very simple. The body of every living thing is made up of millions of tiny units called cells. Cells are too small to be seen with the naked eye. Scientists look at them through microscopes. Under a microscope, you can see an even smaller nucleus at the center of each cell. The nucleus contains the blueprint for life in the form of coded instructions called genes. People inherit genes from their parents. Genes code everything from the color of your eyes to how tall you will be.

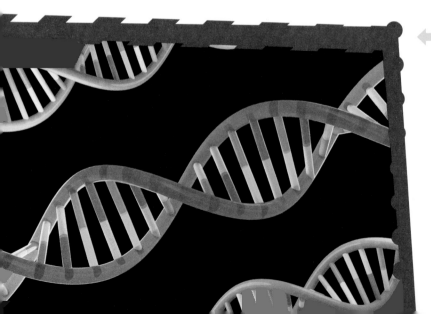

A molecule of DNA looks like a twisted ladder. This shape is called a double helix.

Examining DNA can determine if two people are related. The DNA of these identical twins will be an exact match.

DeoxyriboNucleic Acid, or DNA, is a chemical that carries the code. The only people known to have exactly the same DNA are identical twins. This means that analyzing a sample of DNA evidence can be used for identification. There are some similarities between the DNA profiles of individuals in a family. This means that DNA can also be used to prove whether or not two people are related.

Sources of DNA

DNA can be found in tiny samples of biological evidence such as hairs, bloodstains, or skin cells. Recently, scientists have found a way to obtain a DNA profile from even smaller sources than was previously possible. This is called low copy number (LCN) analysis. However, the results from this method may not always be correct.

TRUE CRIME...

DNA database

In August 1999, two students at Virginia University were asleep when an intruder attacked them, threatened them with a gun, and stole items from their rooms. Traces of saliva found on a beer can at the crime scene were analyzed. However, the DNA profile did not match any of the people the police suspected. Then, in October 1999, a match was found on the police database with the DNA profile of a criminal called Montaret D. Davis. He was put on trial and convicted on the basis of the DNA evidence.

DNA testing

A crime has been committed. The police have a suspect, and they have collected a sample of saliva from his mouth. His DNA will be analyzed. These are the main steps in the testing process.

1. A crime scene investigator notices an object at the crime scene. It may have DNA on it, so she takes a photograph to record the evidence. She puts the sample in a container, seals it and labels it carefully, recording where she found it.

2. The sample is sent to the forensic laboratory. The sample should be kept cool and away from direct sunlight. This is because high temperatures can damage or destroy the DNA.

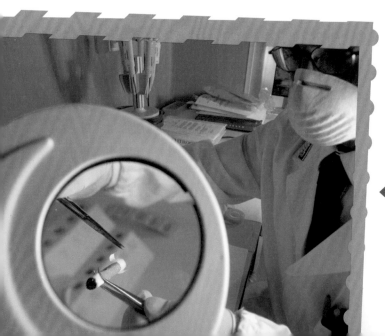

Saliva on the end of a cigarette butt can be used to build up a DNA profile.

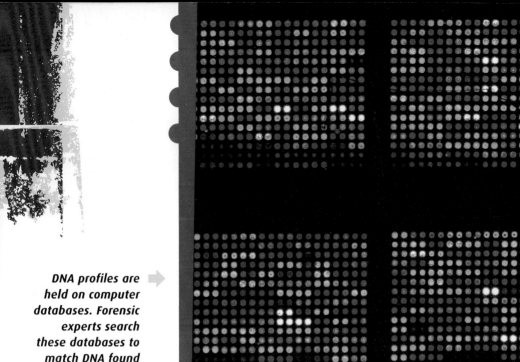

DNA profiles are held on computer databases. Forensic experts search these databases to match DNA found at a crime scene.

3. Back at the laboratory, the DNA is extracted from the sample. The amount of DNA is measured and recorded.

4. The pure sample of DNA is then analyzed. A technique called gel electrophoresis separates the DNA into a column with a series of stripes, like a bar code. This pattern is called the DNA profile.

5. The DNA profile from the crime scene is then compared with the suspect's DNA profile.

6. A match between the suspect's DNA profile and the DNA profile of a crime scene sample may be sufficient evidence to link the suspect to the crime.

7. If there is no suspect, or if the suspect's DNA profile does not match the profile of the sample, police search databases containing DNA profiles of criminals. A match of the sample and a database DNA profile indicates that the person may have been at the crime scene.

Looking at bodies

When a body is found, police need to find out how the person died. Was it the result of illness or an accident, or was it murder or suicide? The body can provide a lot of information to help answer these questions. Bodies are examined by specially trained doctors called forensic pathologists. The examination is called an autopsy or post mortem.

The body is a rich source of evidence. It is stored in a cool mortuary to preserve vital clues.

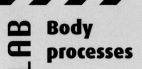

IN THE LAB

Body processes

Some body processes stop after death. For example, a body may have been pulled from a river. Breathing stops at death. If the lungs are full of water, it suggests the person drowned, so this could have been an accident. If their lungs are not full of water, the body entered the water after death, so this is very suspicious.

What can a body reveal?

From an autopsy, a forensic pathologist may be able to figure out when a person died and what killed them. Extra information, such as the type of weapon used in a murder, or whether the victim had been drinking alcohol, can often be found. It may also be possible to tell whether a body was moved after death.

Serious damage to the skull suggests that the person died from a head wound.

How is an autopsy carried out?

Photographs are taken at every step of the autopsy. They may be used as evidence. The first step is to look for clues on the outside of the body. There might be bruises or other injuries to the skin. If a victim tried to fight off an attack, flakes of the attacker's skin might be under the fingernails. Teeth can be compared with dental records to confirm the person's identity.

Next, the internal organs are removed, weighed, and searched for injury. Samples of blood are sent to the forensic laboratory. The blood is tested for drugs, poisons, and other chemicals that might have caused death. Many other tests, such as for an infection or other illness, can be done if it is necessary.

IN DEPTH

Bones speak

This table shows some of the questions that can be answered by examining bones:

Question	From where?	How?
how old was the person when he or she died?	skull	older people have smoother skulls; the bones of a child's skull are not completely joined together
male or female?	skull and pelvis	men have more prominent brows, jawbones, and eye sockets; women have a wider pelvis
how tall?	thigh bone	this is usually about one-quarter of an adult's height
how heavy?	whole skeleton	the heavier the person, the more signs of wear there are
right-handed or left-handed?	arms and shoulders	the dominant side has stronger muscle attachments
occupation?	whole skeleton	job-related changes or damage, for example a trumpet player's teeth may be distorted
ethnic group?	nose shape	differs between groups
violent death?	whole skeleton	signs of injury or struggle, for example damage to the skull, broken bones, bullet damage

Reconstructing the past

When a human body is discovered a long time after death, an ordinary autopsy cannot be done. The remains are too badly decayed. Sometimes only a skeleton remains. Forensic anthropologists are experts in studying these remains. They can still find out a lot about the body to help identify the dead person. Forensic artists can recreate the person's face.

IN DEPTH

A face from the past

Tutankhamun was an Egyptian pharaoh. He ruled between 1336 and 1327 BCE but died when he was only 19 years old. Like all the Egyptian pharaohs, the body of Tutankhamun was preserved as a mummy and buried in a tomb.

Over 3,000 years later, a British archaeologist named Howard Carter discovered the tomb hidden in the Valley of the Kings. When he looked inside, Carter found Tutankhamun's mummy with a beautiful golden mask over his face. Still, no one knew what his actual face looked like.

In 2007, a team of forensic artists from France, Egypt, and the US decided to reconstruct Tutankhamun's face using detailed scans of his skull. The models made show that the pharaoh had rounded cheeks, a sloping nose, and a round chin. At last, we know what Tutankhamun looked like.

Sometimes they make a plaster copy of the skull and stick pieces of plastic onto it at key points such as the nose. The gaps between are filled in with modeling clay. Another way of recreating the body's face is to use a special computer program. Many measurements are taken from the skull and entered into the computer. The program will then create an approximation of the person's face.

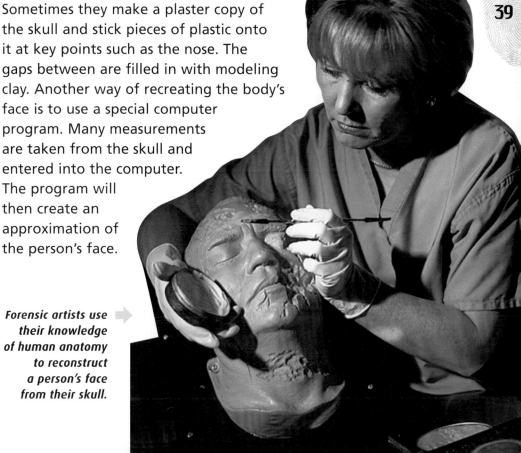

Forensic artists use their knowledge of human anatomy to reconstruct a person's face from their skull.

39

Clues from insects

After a person dies, their body begins to decay. The process can be slowed if the body is kept in a cool place. Otherwise, decay is rapid. As the body decays, insects are attracted to it. Insects can provide clues about the time of death. Insect investigations are done by scientists called forensic entomologists.

Types of insect

The exact insect species involved varies depending on the climate and country. The first to arrive are usually flies. House flies, blowflies, and scavenger flies are just some of the species that appear. They lay eggs on the body. The eggs develop into maggots. Scientists have studied the life cycles of different flies.

Insects help investigators establish the time of death.

They know exactly how many days it takes for the maggots to develop. They can also identify how many generations of maggots and flies have been on the body. This can help them to establish the time of death.

Flies lay their eggs on dead bodies. The eggs hatch into maggots, which feed on the rotting flesh.

Beetles arrive later in the decaying process. Most beetles lay their eggs in the body, and the larvae that emerge feed on the flesh. Hide beetles come late in the decaying process. They feed on dried skin, bone, and hair.

Mites can arrive at any stage to feed on dried skin. Some hitch a ride with the beetles. Moths are some of the last insects to arrive. They feed on hair, and add to the final stages of decay.

Some insects can cause problems for forensic scientists. Some feed on the body, while others eat the eggs and maggots. This makes it hard to figure out the time of death. If the maggots have been eaten, vital information about the generations may be missing.

TRUE CRIME...

Blowfly evidence

The body of a girl was found in Lydney, England, in June 1961. From looking at the level of decay of the body, police thought the murder had taken place six to eight weeks earlier. They were puzzled because several witnesses said they had seen the victim much later than this. But Keith Simpson, the forensic entomologist, said the blowfly maggots he found were just nine to twelve days old. The police used this information to establish the time of death and find the girl's murderer. He was found guilty based on the blowfly evidence.

Chemical clues

Are traces of powder evidence of illegal drugs? Was a fire started by lighting a gas-soaked rag? Chemicals are often found at a crime scene—providing clues about the victim, the suspect, and the way in which the crime was committed.

Forensic toxicologists

Scientists who study chemicals, especially poisons, are called forensic toxicologists. They try to identify the chemicals, their strength, and their effects on people. Forensic toxicologists also study urine or blood samples to test for drugs or poisons.

Simple tests are done first to narrow down the types of chemicals in the sample. Toxicologists then do more detailed tests to find out exactly which substances are present and how much there is of each one. Most samples are tested in two different ways.

Police need to identify the chemicals present at a crime scene. Forensic toxicologists can help the police answer these questions.

Hair evidence

Hair can contain traces of drugs and other substances that have been consumed, either over a long time or in high doses. Hair grows at a rate of about 0.5 inch a month. Testing at a number of different places along the hair's length can indicate when a substance may have been consumed.

Forensic toxicologists test the body for many different drugs, from prescription medicines to illegal drugs. ➡

This is because it is more convincing if the results from two different tests are the same. It shows that the substance really is present in the sample and not the result of a laboratory error.

Poison victim

In suspected poisonings, body samples are taken away for testing. In murder cases, samples are routinely taken and tested as part of the autopsy, even if poison is not suspected. Back at the lab, the samples are treated to extract and purify the poisons. Some poisons are extracted using chemicals, such as chloroform. Techniques called mass spectrometry and chromatography are used to separate different chemicals and then identify them. If a poisonous substance is found in a sample, police know they are looking for a murderer.

TRUE CRIME...

Tylenol

In September 1982, Mary Kellermann took a capsule of a drug called Tylenol™. Soon afterward, she became ill and died. During the next few days, six more people died after taking Tylenol™. Forensic toxicologists analyzed the capsules and found they had been contaminated with a poison called potassium cyanide. The medicine was removed from stores. The toxicologists' work prevented anyone else from getting sick. The police found out what had happened, but they never discovered who had contaminated the capsules.

Careers in forensics

What would it be like to work as a forensic scientist? Probably two facts that everyone would agree on is that every day of their work is different, and that they never know what's going to happen in the laboratory next.

CSIs

Crime scene investigators (CSIs) collect the clues that are later analyzed by forensic specialists. CSIs often work long hours, and they have to deal with some grisly crime scenes. If you don't like the sight of blood, this isn't the job for you! Most CSIs first join a police force. Once they have trained as police officers, they have more specialist training to become a CSI. The entry requirements are different in different places. Many CSIs have a university degree, but many of them do not have a degree.

SALARY CHART

This chart shows what a forensic scientist can expect to earn during the course of their career.

Forensic scientist	Approximate salary
CSI	$46,650—$97,994
Forensic pathologist	$46,650—$97,994
Forensic toxicologist	$47,048—$101,242

Forensic scientists

You will need several important qualities to work in a forensics laboratory. To succeed, you need to be able to:

- work accurately, carrying out scientific tests reliably and to the very highest standards

- be methodical and logical in the way you work, so that you do not mix up samples or results

- be good at mathematics and computing, so that you can analyze your data and write reports

- have a good understanding of one or more basic science subjects.

If this sounds like you, why not think about a career in forensic science? Many colleges and universities offer special degrees in forensic science. Entry requirements vary, but for most having a science background is an advantage.

45

Specialists

Many forensic scientists decide to specialize in one area of forensic science, such as forensic anthropology, pathology, toxicology, serology, or entomology. Some specialists train in their own subject area and then have further training to apply their knowledge to forensic science. Sometimes they learn by working alongside experienced professionals.

For example, a forensic pathologist first trains and works as a doctor. After a few years, he or she can then train to become a forensic pathologist.

Forensic work involves a lot of lab testing, so it helps to have a background in science.

Glossary

antibodies—Chemicals made by the body in response to germs.

autopsy—Examination and dissection of a body after a person has died.

ballistics—The study of guns and bullets.

cast—Model of something.

chromatography—Method used for separating out the different chemicals in a substance.

contaminated—Spoiled by having something unwanted added.

database—Collection of data, or pieces of information.

DNA—Chemical in cells that carries the genetic code passed on from parent to offspring and which determines how someone looks.

encrypted—Written in code.

forensic anthropologist—Scientist who studies bones and skeletons from human remains.

forensic entomologist—Scientist specializing in the study of insects that feed on dead bodies.

forensic pathologist—Doctor who studies tissue and other parts of remains to figure out a history of disease, injury, and cause of death.

forensic scientist—Person who uses science or technology to investigate and establish facts or evidence.

forensic toxicologist—Scientist specializing in the study of poisons in dead bodies.

gel electrophoresis—Method used in the analysis of DNA.

gene—Segment of DNA that contains the code for a trait such as blood type or eye color.

maggot—Wormlike stage in the life cycle of flies.

mass spectrometry—Method used for analyzing and separating chemicals.

mortar—A mixture of material used to glue bricks together in buildings.

organ—Part of the body such as the heart, lungs, or brain.

perimeter—An outer boundary.

pollen—Fine powder made by flowers to fertilize.

porous—Able to absorb liquids.

post mortem—Examination of a body to find out the cause of death.

saliva—Liquid produced by the glands in the mouth.

serology—Study of blood and other body fluids.

Further information

Books

Fridell, Ron. *Forensic Science*. Minneapolis: Lerner Publications Co., 2007.

Rainis, Kenneth G. *Hair, Clothing, and Tire Track Evidence*. Berkeley Heights: Enslow Publishers, Inc., 2006.

Scott, Carey. *Crime Scene Detective*. New York: Dorling Kindersley, 2007.

Web sites

Play games, solve puzzles, take the Special Agent challenge, and much more at the FBI's web site for kids:

www.fbi.gov/kids/6th12th/6th12th.htm

This site features information about forensic and crime scene investigations—plus a mystery to solve:

www.abc.net.au/science/slab/forensic/default.htm

Find a database of forensic science facts, a timeline showing important forensic events, and a game to play, at:

www.virtualmuseum.ca/Exhibitions/Myst/en/rcmp/index.html

Index